UNTIL ALL KNOW

WHOLEHEARTEDLY DEVOTED TO
JESUS AND HIS DREAM

HEATH ADAMSON

GPH®
Gospel Publishing House

Published by Gospel Publishing House
1445 N. Boonville Ave.
Springfield, Missouri 65802

www.myhealthychurch.com

Cover and interior design and formatting by Prodigy Pixel
(www.prodigypixel.com)

ISBN: 978-1-60731-477-6

Printed in the United States of America

21 20 19 18 17 • 1 2 3 4 5

To Ali, Leighton, and Dallon.

For this season and those remaining, the fig tree is always in bloom.

I will teach you hidden lessons from our past—
stories we have heard and known,
stories our ancestors handed down to us.
We will not hide these truths from our children;
we will tell the next generation
about the glorious deeds of the LORD,
about his power and his mighty wonders.
For he issued his laws to Jacob;
he gave his instructions to Israel.
He commanded our ancestors
to teach them to their children,
so the next generation might know them—
even the children not yet born—
and they in turn will teach their own children.
So each generation should set its hope anew on God,
not forgetting his glorious miracles
and obeying his commands.

PSALM 78:2–7, NLT

CONTENTS

CHAPTER ONE

WE BELIEVE IN THE HARVEST

Some places aren't supposed to teem with life. Some places are just too dry.

The Sahel is more than four thousand miles wide and lies just below the Sahara Desert. During May, June, July, and August, twelve months worth of rain will fall and the remaining eight months will be arid and difficult, even deadly. Eight months without rain can have a profound effect on life. Cracks creep across the desert floor. Eyes burn from the dust kicked up thousands of feet in the air by the hot winds. Mirages become commonplace on the horizon. Humans and animals alike crave a drop of water, a bite of food. One wonders how long this area can sustain life.

Del Tarr, a missionary who served fourteen years in West Africa, observed this place firsthand. He knew the dry and dusty roads too well. He recalls how a four-month rainy season meant that farmers grew, harvested, and rationed a year's worth of food in a few short months. Sorghum and milo are two of the major products grown in this remote area of Africa.

Del recalls how the months of October and November were filled with celebration, singing, and dancing. The season of harvest had arrived, and the granaries were filled with food. In the villages, each adult and child enjoyed a luxurious two meals a day. Using ancient stones to grind the grain into flour, the villagers lived off of food consistent with what Del describes as "yesterday's cream of wheat." He goes on to say, "The sticky mush is eaten hot; they roll it into little balls between their fingers, drop it into a bit of sauce and then pop it into their mouths. The meal lies heavy on their stomachs so they can sleep."

With December the villagers know that the luxury of two meals a day will soon come to an end. Grain begins to run low, and families skip breakfast to conserve food. January doesn't bring new hope because, as Tarr explains, "Not one family in fifty is still eating two meals a day."

In February, the one evening meal enjoyed and relished by everyone grows smaller and smaller. In March, many of the children become sick as their immune systems are weakened from malnourishment and hunger. One half of a meal a day just isn't enough.

Here is how Del Tarr graphically described the plight of these people to me:

April is the month that haunts my memory. You hear the babies crying in the twilight. They pass most days with only an evening cup of gruel.

Then, inevitably, it happens. One day a six- or seven-year-old boy comes running to his father, bursting with excitement. "Daddy! Daddy! We've got grain!" he shouts.

The father calms him down and replies, "Son, you know we haven't had grain for weeks."

"Yes, we have!" the boy insists. "Out in the hut where we keep the goats I found a leather sack hanging up on the wall. When I put my hand inside

the sack I felt the grain. There's grain in the sack! Give it to Mommy so she can make flour, and tonight our tummies can sleep!"

The father stands motionless.

"Son, we can't do that," he gently explains. "The seeds in that sack are next year's seed grain. Those seeds are the only thing between us and starvation. We're keeping the grain until the rains come again. Then we'll plant it."

The rains finally arrive in May, and when they do the young boy watches his father take the sack from the wall and do the most unreasonable thing imaginable. Instead of feeding his desperately weakened family, he walks to the field and with tears streaming down his face he takes the precious seed and scatters it in the soil. Why? Because he believes in the harvest.

The dad was willing to plant his most precious seed because he believed in the importance of the harvest. One of my favorite names used in Scripture for Jesus is "a root out of dry ground" (Isaiah 53:2, NKJV). It's interesting to me that when planting His Son in the world, God chose an environment and landscape similar to the Sahel: a place where life isn't supposed to grow and the cries of hungry children fill the night air. That's where God planted the Savior. Jesus breathes life over the dead places. He causes things to grow when they aren't supposed to. Why? Because to Him, things aren't necessarily dead; they're merely dormant. This is what Moses experienced in another desert.

A young Hebrew child, Moses was supposed to die. Pharaoh issued the edict for the murder of the innocents, and soldiers killed the children. It was God's providence that Moses, discovered by Pharaoh's daughter on the banks of the river, would grow up in the palace of the leader who had issued the order for his death. Moses became accustomed to the ways of royalty during a time when Egypt enslaved the Hebrews for over four hundred years. Ironically, Moses was the only Hebrew in the land who understood how royalty lived.

At the age of forty, Moses murdered an Egyptian and someone discovered his crime. In order to save his own life, he fled the luxury and pomp and circumstance in Egypt and vanished into the Sinai Peninsula. For forty years, Moses tended sheep under the hot sun. He married and began a family. The past he had tried to bury in the sand became a fading memory.

At the age of eighty, on a day like all other days, Moses watched the sun come up over the great Horeb range of mountains. The shadow from Mount Horeb brought relief from the heat as the desert winds churned up dust like the dry soil of the African Sahel. On that day, as Moses walked past a bush, he noticed something that forever altered his understanding of God and changed the way the next generation would understand God.

Now Moses was keeping the flock of his father-in-law, Jethro, the priest of Midian, and he led his flock to the west side of the wilderness and came to Horeb, the mountain of God. And the angel of the Lord appeared to him in a flame of fire out of the midst of a bush. He looked, and behold, the bush was burning, yet it was not consumed. And Moses said, "I will turn aside to see this great sight, why the bush is not burned." When the Lord saw that he turned aside to see, God called to him out of the bush, "Moses, Moses!" And he said, "Here I am." Then he said, "Do not come near; take your sandals off your feet, for the place on which you are standing is holy ground." And he said, "I am the God of your father, the God of Abraham, the God of Isaac, and the God of Jacob." And Moses hid his face, for he was afraid to look at God.

Then the LORD said, "I have surely seen the affliction of my people who are in Egypt and have heard their cry because of their taskmasters. I know their sufferings, and I have come down to deliver them out of the hand of the Egyptians and to bring them up out of that land to a good and broad land, a land flowing with milk and honey, to the place of the Canaanites, the Hittites, the Amorites, the Perizzites, the Hivites, and the Jebusites." (Exodus 3:1–8, ESV)

I write about this event in my book *The Bush Always Burns*. The verses explain that Moses "turned aside to see" and *then* God spoke. There are some aspects of the kingdom that God waits to share with us until He sees the effort we make. Proverbs 25:2 (ESV) says "It is the glory of God to conceal things, but the glory of kings is to search things out." Moses searched out why the bush was aflame but was not consumed . . . and *then* God spoke. When God has something to say, we want to posture our hearts and do whatever it takes to turn aside.

Moses saw that the bush was on fire but was not consumed. The Hebrew word for "saw" is *ra'ah,* which can mean "to see with the eyes of the soul." For centuries rabbis commented on this Scripture saying that the bush had been on fire for quite some time and Moses just happened to slow down long enough to notice. To notice what? That his world was aflame with the divine. It makes you wonder how many other people walked past the bush unaware that God was there . . . waiting . . . with something to say.

It was in the desert, the African desert ironically, that the dry place became fertile with God's voice. When He speaks, dead things come to life.

God heard the cry of His people in Egypt and responded. His solution? A person named Moses. Someone who was willing to turn aside and see what God was doing even in an environment that seemed empty of life and void of anything supernatural.

Some places just aren't supposed to have life. Some places are just too dry . . . until God shows up. In the Garden of Eden God took a handful of dirt, breathed on it, and humanity was formed. God spoke the worlds into existence, but He saved His very breath for us. It was in the dry place near Mount Horeb that God spoke and summoned Moses to become a scribe of the future for an entire nation. It was in the dry place of the Sahel where an earthly father dared to believe in the importance of planting seed, for he knew the harvest would come one day.

Just as in the life of Moses, an entire generation of young people need to know that even in the dry and barren places, their world is aflame with the divine. There is a generation of young people, similar to the young boy in the Sahel, who don't fully understand the importance of the harvest nor do they know for sure that the rains will come again. There is a generation of young people who need someone to take them by the hand and guide them, someone who has lived through the dry season, felt the dust in their face, and listened to the choir of hungry children while believing that a better day can and will come. There is a generation of young people who need someone who has traversed the great deserts and seen God at work to teach them courage and faith and hope.

Many people look at the dry spiritual climate of our nation, this generation, and our world and feel that the rain of God's powerful blessings will never come again. Perhaps you are one of them. You look at the moral demise of this world and wonder where God is. Aspects of your own spiritual life may feel dry and even dead. Perhaps you are concerned for your children and grandchildren, your friends at school, your spouse, or your coworkers as they cry out for spiritual restoration and relief and find none, just like the children of the Sahel cry out for rain and find only more dry, hot dust.

Let me remind you that we pray to a God who intentionally chooses to plant His kingdom in the driest of soils. We serve a God who called Elijah to the brook in the midst of the great drought only to cause the brook to dry up. Why? God knew that one day Elijah would see a cloud the size of a man's hand on the horizon and rain would fall. We serve a God who can bring life out of nothing. We serve a God who chooses to take us by the hand, just like the dad took the hand of his son in the Sahel, and journey with us as we take what is most precious to us (our time, our families, our dreams, our finances, and our reputations) and plant it in the soil of eternity, for that soil *always* produces a harvest.

God instructs us to "ask the LORD for rain in the springtime" (Zechariah 10:1). Note that we are to ask for rain in the springtime, when it's already supposed to rain. Just because it's raining, don't assume you'll get wet. This Scripture challenges me to find a spiritually dry place, stand right in the middle of it, and pray for rain. Jude 1:12 describes those who claim to be Christians but have no relationship with Jesus as "clouds without rain." We are living in a spiritually dry time where we discover what we truly believe. For those who hide in a subculture of holiness, the seed in the dry ground is dead. Those who use relevance as an excuse for compromise are consuming the seeds in the bag in the shed to stave off temporary hunger pains. For those who understand that God is planting His church in dry ground in order to bring life from what is dead, this is a season to pray for rain—and this is a season to plant seed.

If you're reading this book, it's because you believe in the law of the harvest. You believe in the harvest Jesus spoke of in Matthew 28. You believe that one day God will send the rain again. And, like the father in the Sahel, you believe this generation needs someone to explain why we live our lives with the eternal harvest in mind. As I travel frequently and interact with men and women of all ages, I see three specific seeds we are to plant for this moment in history: the seed of the gospel, the seed of the Holy Spirit, and the seed of the mission. Rather than criticizing the ground for being dry and the skies for being empty of rain, let's choose to follow God's example in Isaiah 53:2 for we know one day, and one day very soon, the harvest is coming.

In doing this, we become scribes of the future: we write the next chapter of God's story with Him. In doing this, we plant seed in the soil of eternity. In doing this, we teach that young boy who stood on African soil how to take his son and daughter by the hand and explain why what we don't see is more real than the dry, dusty desert we see all around us.

STUDENT QUESTIONS:

- When you look at your school, friends, or community, do you see dry and barren places?
- Would you choose to plant a seed in the desert? Why or why not?
- Identify three names or areas that appear spiritually dry. Would you be willing to stand in the middle of the desert and pray for rain?

LEADER QUESTIONS:

- When you look at the landscape of the next generation, what do you see?
- Have you stopped to consider that you are part of God's solution? As a parent or leader, what do you feel is your role in preparing the next generation?
- The three seeds we are planting are the gospel, the Spirit, and the mission of God. Do you feel like these seeds are flourishing in your life? Why or why not?
- Pray about the students and areas where you could plant these seeds. What are your next steps?

CHAPTER TWO

WE WILL NEVER FORGET

Seriously? They didn't know? Someone didn't take them by the hand and show them?

Julio Diaz comes to mind when I think of how powerful it is to take someone by the hand and show them the most excellent way.

Diaz was a thirty-one-year-old social worker from the Bronx with a daily routine. Every night on his way home from work he got off the New York subway one stop early so he could eat at his favorite diner around the corner. One night in 2012, like usual Julio stepped off the train onto a virtually empty platform where he was greeted with something he didn't expect. There, standing on the platform, was a teenage boy with a knife, who demanded Julio give him his wallet.

On the one hand, the decision for Julio was easy. Of course, he would hand over his wallet. It wouldn't make sense to risk his life for the sake of the cash in his wallet. But rather than just simply hand over his wallet, Julio decided to do something else, too. He offered his coat to the young man.

"If you're going to risk your freedom for just a few dollars, you must really need the money," Julio said to the boy. "Here, go ahead, take my coat, too. Otherwise you'll freeze out here." The young man looked at him, stunned.

"In fact," Julio suggested, "why don't you come with me? I'm about to walk down the street and get a bite to eat. I'll buy you dinner." So the young man followed Julio down the street to the diner where Julio always ate.

While at dinner, practically every person in the restaurant came by the table to say hello to Julio. The waiters said hello. Cooks came out from the kitchen to say hello. Even the dishwasher came out to shake hands with Julio and say hello. The young man was shocked.

"Man, you know everyone in this place! Do you own it or something?"

"No. I just come here a lot."

"But you even said hello to the dishwasher," the young man said in amazement.

"Yeah," Julio replied. "Didn't anyone ever teach you to treat people with respect, regardless of their position?"

"Of course. I just didn't think anyone actually lived that way."

Julio and the young man finished their dinner, and after the waiter had dropped the bill and cleared away their plates, Julio looked right into the eyes of the young man. "Look," he told him, "you have my wallet. So, if you want to give it back to me, I can treat you to dinner. But if you want to keep it, you're going to have to pay."

Without hesitating, the young man handed the wallet back to Julio. After paying for the dinner, Julio convinced the young man to trade him the knife for twenty bucks, and then sent the young man back into the night, a changed person. That's the power of one person taking someone by the hand and showing them the right way to live.

No one showed the people the right way to live in Judges 2.

A GENERATION THAT DID NOT KNOW GOD

Imagine what it was like to live in a home where your parents or grandparents had stood on the shore of the Red Sea when God parted the waters. The Hebrews walked across on dry ground while the king's guard from Egypt pursued them (Exodus 14). I have read that up to fifty thousand horsemen and two hundred thousand of Pharaoh's foot soldiers were killed that day while millions of Hebrews were set free from human trafficking and walked toward freedom. Moses encouraged the children of Israel to stand still and watch God deliver them. God responded with "Why are you crying out to me? Tell the Israelites to move on" (Exodus 14:15). There's a time to pray and there's a time to obey. "Moses stretched out his hand over the sea and all that night the LORD drove the sea back with a strong east wind and turned it into dry land" (v. 21). God parted the Sea. Some scholars tell us the walls of water would have been over fourteen stories tall. The Israelites watched as mankind partnered with the divine to change the course of history. What a remarkable and truly unforgettable experience!

As the people traveled in the desert, God miraculously caused water to gush from a rock (Exodus 17). In a place similar to the Sahel, God supernaturally irrigated the land. The people watched as God met with Moses, "face to face as a man speaks with his friend" (Exodus 33:11, NCV). They witnessed the tangible presence of God in a cloud during the day and a burning pillar of fire by night. God supplied their food every day through the form of manna and eventually other sources such as wild quail. The glory of God rested in the tabernacle. I can only imagine what it felt like to see and be near God in that way. They saw Moses' face glow from being in the presence of God (Exodus

34:34–35). Someone once said that as we read Scripture, it's important that we don't read what we believe; rather, we must believe what we read. These are stories for "believing believers." He is the same God today as He's always been (Hebrews 13:8).

When Moses died, God chose Joshua to lead the people. As a young man, Joshua had walked closely with Moses and had witnessed firsthand many things others would never have seen. One of my favorite descriptions of Joshua is recorded in Exodus 33:11: "Thus the LORD used to speak to Moses face to face, as a man speaks to his friend. When Moses turned again into the camp, his assistant Joshua the son of Nun, a young man, would not depart from the tent" (ESV). Another translation states that Joshua "stayed behind a little longer." When no one else was looking, Joshua remained in God's presence. Perhaps that's why God chose Joshua to replace the great Moses and continue leading God's people toward the Promised Land.

God encouraged Joshua to be strong and courageous, as the task in front of him would require just as much faith and belief as in the days of Moses. The same people who witnessed the glowing face of Moses had children who witnessed the walls of Jericho crumble. Jericho was six miles north of the Dead Sea. It was an oasis built on an underground spring in the middle of the desert. It was the center of ancient Canaan; a road traveling from the east to the west made it a gateway of trade between the Transjordan and the highlands of Judah. Built on a mound seventy feet high, it was fortified with double walls.[1]

The outer wall, based on archaeological evidence, was about twenty-six feet high and sat atop a retaining wall that was ten to fifteen feet high. It was six feet thick. At the top of the earthen embankment sat the inner wall, which was forty-six feet above the ground. The underground spring provided ample water for the city and according to Joshua 3:15, the harvest had just taken place. There was plenty of food and water for the citizens of Jericho to withstand a siege. For all practical purposes, Jericho could never fall. Joshua 6 records how the God who brought water from the rock in the desert tore down walls that no one could break. On the seventh day, as the Israelites marched around the city they saw the vast walls crumble. God gave the city into their hands. What a truly unforgettable experience! I can only imagine the stories fathers told their children as they lingered around the campfires in Canaan.

Joshua led the Israelites to one victory after another. They continued to witness God's provision and power. I have been told that Joshua was such an amazing general that his military strategies are still discussed today in some of the world's finest military academies. But some things that are unforgettable can be forgotten.

And the people served the LORD all the days of Joshua, and all the days of the elders who outlived Joshua, who had seen all the great work that the LORD had done for Israel. And Joshua the son of Nun, the servant of the LORD, died at the age of 110 years. And they buried him within the boundaries of his inheritance in Timnath-heres, in the hill country of Ephraim, north of the mountain of Gaash. And all that generation also were gathered to their fathers. *And there arose another generation after them who did not know the LORD or the work that he had done for Israel.* (Judges 2:7–10, ESV, emphasis added)

This is unthinkable! How does a child grow up in a home with parents or grandparents who had firsthand knowledge of the miracles and wonders God performed in the days of Moses and Joshua without knowing about God? The Bible says they "did not know the LORD." This is a travesty! The most basic human right in the world is the right to know Jesus. It doesn't stop there, though. It says they did not know "the work that [God] had done for Israel." They didn't know the story of the great Jericho walls falling down. They didn't know the story of the Red Sea parting. They didn't know the story of God's grace in providing manna on the desert floor. And worst of all, they didn't even know the miracle-working God behind all the miracles.

How do you sit at a campfire with your family and fail to mention these things? History shows us that while the children played in the fields of Canaan, oblivious to who the God of Israel was, the adults were off fighting in God's conquest. Like Joshua's generation, we should be engaged and surrendered to the purposes of God but *not* at the expense of teaching the next generation about God and His works. This perhaps explains God's heartbeat as recorded through Asaph in Psalm 78:

> I will utter dark sayings from of old, things that we have heard and known, that our fathers have told us. We will not hide them from their children, but tell to the coming generation the glorious deeds of the LORD, and his might, and the wonders that he has done. He established a testimony in Jacob and appointed a law in Israel, which he commanded our fathers to teach to their children, that the next generation might know them. (Psalm 78:2–6, ESV)

We stand on the edge of yet another generation of young people who must know God as well as His works. These two are inseparable: His works reveal His character. We know what it's like to see God provide for our needs. We were there when He took an impossible situation and turned it around. We know His miracles and presence are as real and accessible as ever. That's why it's up to us to take the next generation by the hand and walk together in full awareness of the power of God. This is nothing new. At the epicenter of revival during the days of Azusa Street, a radical and prophetic community of people dared to know God and His works. Our church movement was born as a faith community out of an encounter with Him, and the next generation was already there.

A MULTIGENERATIONAL REVIVAL

"Either shut it down or rent a place like an auditorium," the police officer cautioned William Seymour. Richard and Ruth Asbury had opened up their home on Bonnie Brae Street for Seymour to hold revival meetings. Neighbors summoned the police who asked Seymour to shut down the meeting because innocent people were falling down in the streets, blocks away, and speaking in tongues without knowing what was happening to them. It was 1906 and the prayers arising from the home on Bonnie Brae were creating a traffic jam of horses and buggies.

Seymour had been invited from Houston to pastor a church in Los Angeles. His first sermon on a Sunday morning was on the Holy Spirit. When he arrived back at the church that evening, the doors were chained and a note was posted on the door: "You are fired. We don't want that strange stuff." Richard Asbury was a part of this church, but he didn't agree with their decision to fire Seymour. That's why he opened up his home for prayer meetings.

That night, when the police officer warned Seymour, the preacher knew he needed to find a solution. He needed a location and money. God instructed Seymour to get on a trolley car and travel to Pasadena as soon as the service was over. Seymour was unsure where he would end up. He knew that by the time he arrived in Pasadena, it would be dark, forcing him to break the law. The sundown law prevented anyone of color from walking the streets in Pasadena after dark.

Seymour left the trolley car and was led step-by-step by the Holy Spirit until he arrived at an apartment. There, a group of Baptists were praying for the baptism in the Holy Spirit. Seymour knocked on the door and startled the group, who were about to call the police. A seventeen-year-old girl named Sister Carney answered the door and there she saw a half-blind, African American man. "Can I help you?"

That group of ladies didn't know it but after several months of fervent prayer for revival God was going to answer their prayers in a most unusual way. "You're praying for revival, right?" Seymour inquired of them. He continued, "I'm the man God has sent to preach the revival." The ladies invited him in. They prayed, he preached, and they took up an offering to pay for use of a building on Azusa Street. That prayer gathering of ladies was initially started by Sister Carney, who was baptized in the Holy Spirit at the age of fifteen in 1904. She had influenced her Baptist friends to hunger for more of God, and after two years of prayer, Seymour came to their door.[2]

There was a hunger and desperation for the presence of God in all generations before the Azusa Street revival began. I would argue that it began long before anyone recognized it. Often, the most significant shifts in the kingdom go unrecognized or ignored until they are publicly celebrated. For years, all across Los Angeles, people gathered in homes and cried out to God to know Him and His works. People didn't use relevance as an excuse to compromise their longings nor did they use holiness as an excuse to hide in a religious subculture. Their lives were built on a foundation of prayer and holiness as well as an openness to what surprises God might provide. A teenager named Sister Carney was at the center of it all.

Out of this spiritual awakening, to which we owe much as a faith community, grew an intense burden to ensure the next generation knew God and His works. The September 25, 1926, issue of the *Pentecostal Evangel* included "an appeal to the young people" and stressed their important role in the kingdom of God. It stated: "It is the natural prerogative of young people to do the aggressive work."

Just a few years after the outpouring of the Spirit in the days of Azusa, there were indicators that the concerns for the next generation to know God and His works were growing. In a memoir of Ralph Harris (the first national Youth director of the General Council of the Assemblies of God) written in June 1981, he stated the concern leadership had in the 1940s. "My first shock came when I talked with certain leaders. . . . They stated their view that the pattern of history could not be changed, that throughout church history movements have arisen, flourished for a while, then became worldly, lost the original vision, losing out spiritually, becoming just an organization.

This is what happened to the Methodists." As Ralph Harris prayed and began thinking of how the next generation could know God and His works, he came to this realization: "The hope for the future still lies with the young people of our Movement, and a repetition of the experiences that brought our Movement into existence."

And what were those experiences? Well, it's quite simple. The generations, races, and genders committed to pray together, serve together, and live together in a way that glorified God. This commitment was so deep that at a time when racism divided our nation, a Los Angeles newspaper said "the color line was washed away in the blood line." At a time when females weren't considered for leadership, those present at Azusa recognized the deep value and gifts present in the women, and our history is written through the hands of godly men and women. At a time when poverty and wealth divided people on the streets, everyone came together and found commonality in Jesus.

They didn't believe that Jesus was a way or even a preferred way but that He was the only way to the Father (John 14:6). They were committed to the gospel. They held a deep conviction that the purpose of God we are to fulfill in our generation is so significant that we cannot do it on our own. The power of the Holy Spirit isn't a luxury but a necessity. It is still true that the work of the Lord is not accomplished by might, nor by power, but by His Spirit (Zechariah 4:6).

Those early revivalists held a deep conviction that Matthew 28 isn't a great suggestion but the great mission of God for His church. People gave their lives to take the gospel to the unreached and surrendered their lives to demonstrate the gospel in their neighborhoods at home.

THE GOSPEL, THE SPIRIT, THE MISSION

It falls to us to take the next generation by the hand and explain why the harvest is important and ensure the right seeds are planted. May our memories never be greater than our dreams. May we refuse to sabotage or abort the miraculous works of God in the next generation because we are preoccupied with fighting our own spiritual battles as the people were in Judges 2. Let us pray for prayer and repent of our repentance (as the Puritans would say). Let us never confuse prayer with procrastination. There's a time to pray and a time to obey. Let us be accused of doing all we can so that God and His works are known. He will be known and only known through the gospel. His works will be demonstrated through us by the power of the Spirit. His purpose, which is the mission, will unite us.

I'm asking you to take the next generation by the hand and ensure three significant seeds are planted in the soil of tomorrow . . . that they might know Christ and the mighty power of the Holy Spirit. In case you are wondering if the seeds can grow in this spiritually dry culture of ours, just remember how Isaiah described Jesus: He was a *"root out of dry ground."*

STUDENT QUESTIONS:

- What is something practical that someone has done for you that's made an impact?
- Sometimes the most spiritual moments happen because someone is faithful with what's in front of them. Are you aware of and listening to the Holy Spirit's guidance in your life as you walk through your school and spend time with friends?
- Think of your relationship with God. How are you continuing to grow in your knowledge of Him and His works?
- Are you willing to be faithful when no one is watching?

LEADER QUESTIONS:

- What are some reasons a generation can grow up and not know God or His works?
- What is something practical that you have done that impacted a student in your home or your ministry? If you can't think of anything, now is the time to start.
- Do you believe your students have the ability to pray like Sister Carney? How are you encouraging them to be faithful when no one is watching?
- Our movement was born out of encounter with the Holy Spirit. As you lead, are you open to encountering Jesus through the work of the Holy Spirit? How are you encouraging your students to be open to an encounter with Jesus?

CHAPTER THREE

THE SEED OF THE GOSPEL

What you see is not all there is.

It was September 1999. As the leaves began to change color, Joan Murray, a forty-seven-year-old bank executive in North Carolina, was about to jump out of an airplane 14,500 feet from the ground. She wasn't nervous, as dozens of times before she had done the same thing. Knowing when and how to open her parachute was something Joan Murray had mastered. But heading toward the ground at eighty miles per hour and having both her parachute and reserve chute fail to open was *not* something she had ever planned for. Once her reserve chute finally opened a mere seven hundred feet from the ground, it was too late. Joan hit the ground with a force that shattered the right side of her body, even knocking out the fillings in her teeth.

She lay on the ground, her semiconscious body wracked with pain. When the paramedics arrived and quickly raced her to a nearby hospital, the damage to her body was inestimable. Her life lay in the balance. She lay in a coma for two weeks at the Carolinas Medical Center in Charlotte, North Carolina. Her body retained fluid as she swelled from her injuries. Her 115-pound body was unrecognizable, but that wasn't the only thing.

Where did all the stings and bites come from? There were over two hundred of them.

Ironically, when Joan Murray hit the ground, she landed on top of a massive colony of fire ants. Imagine laying on the ground wondering whether or not you will even survive, while being stung by fire ants. Those stings, however, doctors estimate may well have saved her life. Believe it or not, health professionals assert the ant stings shocked her heart with the perfect amount of electricity to keep her alive.

Joan Murray recovered in the hospital and after six weeks returned home. While her recovery was long and painful, in July 2001 she went for her thirty-seventh skydiving jump . . . and landed perfectly.[3]

No one intentionally lays on top of a mound covered in fire ants. As Joan soared to the earth on that horrific day, the very ants she couldn't see, which were a circumstance she would normally choose to avoid, became the bridge to her tomorrow. What was unseen brought back her life.

In a similar way, there are so many things going on behind the scene in each of our lives that we are not aware of. What you see is not all there is. The unseen is often where true life emerges. And the very circumstance you would choose to avoid, like the dry Sahel or the lonely subway where Julio Diaz encountered a thief, may well be the circumstance God uses to impact you, your family, your generation, and His church in a positive way.

Just ask Daniel.

.

DEVOTED TO GOD

Daniel, along with many others, grew up with a unique understanding of the world. The Jews were the only religion we know of in Mesopotamia that believed in one God who sovereignly rules and reigns. The enemies of Israel feared this group of people as rumors of the cloud by day and pillar of fire by night spread throughout the land. And the walls of Jericho that fell still echoed after many generations. The nations throughout the land knew that God was with Israel. One of the evidences of this was Solomon's temple. As little children ran down the hills and adolescents climbed up the valleys, they saw this place where the tangible presence of God dwelled. God was the Strong One and He was among His people. In the temple, the priests made sacrifices and prayed for peace between God and His people. Without the temple, it was not possible to offer sacrifices for sins. Without the temple, there was no sobering reminder of God's power and love. Without the temple, there was no protection and guidance from God. At least that's what the people thought; but they learned just how wrong they were.

Historians tell us that around 586 BC the Babylonian armies invaded ancient Israel and destroyed the temple. For all practical purposes, many people considered the great God Jehovah dead or at least no longer interested in His people. It was more than the destruction of a building. It was a complete contradiction of what Scripture taught about God and the circumstances Daniel found himself in. What do you do when the situation you are in contradicts what you know about God from His Word? You trust Him and you rely on the fact that what you see is not all there is. Like Joan Murray, you are sustained by something you don't see.

Daniel may have witnessed the murder of his family and friends. We don't know for certain. What we do know is that he, along with many other Israelites, lost all that was familiar to them and became victims of human trafficking. They weren't refugees; they were hostages. Historians and archaeologists tell us that in the center of the great city of Babylon stood a 650-foot ziggurat that resembled the tower of Babel. It would have caught Daniel's attention when he came into the city. It was much larger than Solomon's temple. It was where the Babylonians honored their gods. You could only get into Babylon if you were invited . . . or escorted as a hostage. Two hundred square miles of state-of-the-art buildings and entertainment centers dominated the city. The outer walls were approximately twenty-two feet thick and ninety feet high. The Euphrates River flowed through the heart of the city and the leaders had taken care to stockpile decades' worth of food. The armies of Babylon were highly trained. The city was indestructible. The culture had no room for the God of Israel. In fact, the culture was hostile toward Him.

Where was God when Daniel was taken captive?

The Babylonians attacked the identity of Daniel and the identity of his God. They threw away his Jewish name and gave him a new Babylonian name. Names were synonymous with identity and purpose. Every time someone called his name, it seemed that Daniel was being torn away from the God who created him. At least, that's what the ancient Babylonians wanted him to think. Does this sound familiar? In our culture, there is a concerted effort to attack a person's identity. People no longer struggle alone with who the true God is. Now, many struggle with who they are as individuals. People ask questions like, "What gender am I?" and "Does God even recognize me?" Daniel learned how to remain true to who he was regardless of his circumstances. How? He devoted himself to God. "Now when Daniel learned that the decree had been published, he went home to his upstairs room where the windows opened toward Jerusalem. Three times a day he got down on his knees and prayed, giving thanks to his God, just as he had done before." (Daniel 6:10)

The circumstances and culture of Babylon assaulted Daniel's faith. The same king who was responsible for destroying the temple in Israel and killing Daniel's family, heritage, and culture, now tried to destroy the memory of Daniel's God. King Nebuchadnezzar commanded Daniel and the other Jewish abductees to worship the same gods in the same ways as the Babylonians. Prayer became taboo. Scripture was no longer honored or revered. But Daniel didn't allow his circumstances to dictate what he knew to be true about God.

His freedom, rights, and life were put to the test. You may be familiar with the Bible story of Daniel being thrown into a den with lions. It isn't a fairy tale or clever story told in preschools. It really happened. Daniel was criticized, mocked, persecuted, and almost murdered because of his faithful relationship with God. Daniel suffered immensely in a culture that had no room for clear moral standards. Yet God rescued Daniel over and over again. It's interesting to me that God didn't prevent Daniel from being thrown into the lions' den, but in the *midst* of the lions' den God demonstrated His power and His care for Daniel.

Nobody wakes up in the morning and hopes to be placed in an environment filled with hostility and danger. Daniel didn't long for the days when his faith would not only be unpopular but unwanted. Like Joan Murray, Daniel was in a desperate place, but there was more going on behind the scenes than Daniel could see. Like Sister Carney at that obscure prayer meeting before the Azusa Street revival bloomed, Daniel was on the verge of something profound, and he didn't know it. Sometimes the very circumstances we choose to avoid or the difficult circumstances that come into our lives are the things that bring the most honor to God. History is "His Story."

Daniel caught a glimpse of how God is present and at work even in difficult times. Daniel 4 records one of the most remarkable and unbelievable stories in all of Scripture. King Nebuchadnezzar, the king who had ordered the destruction of Jerusalem, had a dream. When no one else could interpret the dream for the king, Daniel was able to explain the dream. There are people, like Daniel, who live lives of hidden commitment to God. Just because someone isn't noticed and celebrated consistently here on the earth doesn't mean heaven is unaware of their lives. This world is filled with people whose hearts are committed to God. At just the right time, that commitment and His purpose collide—and that changes everything.

Daniel risked his life when he explained the dream to the king. After all, it wasn't a dream people like to have:

"You shall be driven from among men, and your dwelling shall be with the beasts of the field. You shall be made to eat grass like an ox, and you shall be wet with the dew of heaven, and seven periods of time shall pass over you, till you know that the Most High rules the kingdom of men and gives it to whom he will. And as it was commanded to leave the stump of the roots of the tree, your kingdom shall be confirmed for you from the time that you know that Heaven rules." (Daniel 4:25–26, ESV)

Daniel basically said that King Nebuchadnezzar would end up leaving his palace and living with animals in the fields. The king who lived in luxury would no longer feast at his own table; rather, he would become insane and eat grass like an ox. How long would this last? Not a day or a week, but for seven years. And, according to both the biblical record and non-biblical records, it happened exactly as Daniel said it would. "While the words were still in the king's mouth, there fell a voice from heaven, 'O King Nebuchadnezzar, to you it is spoken: The kingdom has departed from you'" (Daniel 4:31, ESV).

At the end of the seven-year period, the king who sat on top of the world at one time and crawled upon it the next, was awakened and spiritually resurrected:

"At the end of the days I, Nebuchadnezzar, lifted my eyes to heaven, and my reason returned to me, and I blessed the Most High, and praised and honored him who lives forever, for his dominion is an everlasting dominion, and his kingdom endures from generation to generation; all the inhabitants of the earth are accounted as nothing, and he does according to his will among the host of heaven and among the inhabitants of the earth; and none can stay his hand or say to him, 'What have you done?' At the same time my reason returned to me, and for the glory of my kingdom, my majesty and splendor returned to me. My counselors and my lords sought me, and I was established in my kingdom, and still more greatness was added to me. Now I, Nebuchadnezzar, praise and extol and honor the King of heaven, for all his works are right and his ways are just; and those who walk in pride he is able to humble." (Daniel 4:34-37, ESV)

Nebuchadnezzar experienced a miracle. Not only did he have proof that God was real and can heal, but the king experienced an even greater miracle. He was spiritually resurrected. In the midst of a culture that didn't value human life and consistently violated human rights, where moral standards were hard to find and sexual promiscuity and human trafficking were rampant, where those in poverty grew increasingly poor while the wealthy grew ever richer, and the truth was hard to find, God had an ultimate priority. He chose to reveal Himself to Nebuchadnezzar—first and foremost because even the king had a spiritual need that no one but God could meet.

We live in a world where people die from a lack of pure drinking water. This is tragic and God cares about this human right.

People are sold into slavery every day in our modern and educated culture. This should not happen. God wants human trafficking to end.

It's wrong for anyone created in God's image to be disdained or mistreated because of the color of his or her skin or gender.

God cares about human rights today just as He did in Daniel's day. And while God summons His people to engage in community and serve humanity, the greatest injustice in all the earth isn't for someone to be sold as a slave or to lack clean drinking water. These things are a travesty, and we must not become numb to them. God cares about human rights. However, God's plan is that all would know Him personally. The only way to know God personally is through the path He has laid before us. For this reason, the greatest tragedy in all the earth is for someone to live and die without knowing God.

Although God cared about the suffering in ancient Babylon and He certainly didn't approve of the immoral practices rampant in that society, His ultimate concern was for the spiritual state of the people. He demonstrated this by reaching out to Nebuchadnezzar and revealing Himself to the king. If we preach a gospel apart from justice and compassion, we preach a gospel Jesus never preached. God didn't just forgive Nebuchadnezzar, He healed his body and restored his mental health. If all we do is focus on justice and compassion apart from the gospel, we merely offer people a better brand of eternal misery.

God had compassion on Nebuchadnezzar first and foremost by breathing life into the king's dead soul. A God who takes initiative and reaches out to us in our spiritually dead condition is good news to us all. It is His story written over centuries on both the pages of Scripture and the tablet of the human heart. Being at peace with God by coming alive spiritually isn't the only priority of heaven for us in this life, but it is the first and foremost priority.

In the midst of our culture today we see many similarities between our spiritual story and Daniel's. What we see, however, is not all there is. There's much more going on behind the scenes than we can fathom. And what we don't see is often much more real than what we do see.

Solomon wrote in Ecclesiastes that eternity is written on the hearts of humanity. Even in the spiritual barrenness of Babylon, God saw eternity written on the heart of King Nebuchadnezzar. When you look at your family, friends, school, neighborhood, nation, or world, what do you see? Some see confusion and pain while others see ground as spiritually dry as the Sahel. What does God see? He sees eternity written with His own hand upon the hearts of everyone— including those who deny Him or ignore Him. He doesn't give up on them, and He doesn't give up on us. In our dry, spiritual wasteland, He planted His Son, Jesus. And Jesus is the Word who became flesh (John 1:1,14). When God wanted to transform this world, He chose to plant a seed known as the gospel. The root out of dry ground must be planted in this generation as well as there are many who are simply too ashamed to come home. Just like Christina.

THE GOSPEL IS GRACE

In *No Wonder They Call Him the Savior*, author Max Lucado tells the story of Maria and her daughter Christina. Longing to leave her poor Brazilian neighborhood, Christina wanted to see the world. Discontent living at home with only a pallet on the floor, a washbasin, and a wood-burning stove, she dreamed of a better life in the city. One morning she ran away, breaking her mother's heart. Her mother knew what life on the streets would be like for her young, attractive daughter, so Maria quickly packed to go find her daughter. On her way to the bus stop, she went to a drugstore to get one last thing—pictures. She sat in the photograph booth, closed the curtain, and spent all the money she could on pictures of herself. With her purse full of small black-and-white photos, she got on the next bus to Rio de Janeiro.

Maria knew Christina had no way of earning money. She also knew that her daughter was too stubborn to give up. Maria began her search. Bars, hotels, nightclubs, any place with a reputation for street walkers or prostitutes. At each place she left her picture—taped on a bathroom mirror, tacked to a hotel bulletin board, or fastened to a corner phone booth. On the back of each photo she wrote a note. It wasn't too long before Maria's money and pictures ran out and she had to go home. The tired mother cried as the bus began its long journey back to her small village.

A few weeks later, Christina walked down the stairs in a seedy hotel. Her young face was tired. Her brown eyes no longer danced with youth but spoke of pain and fear. Her laughter was broken. Her dream had become a nightmare. A thousand times she had longed to trade all those countless beds for the secure pallet in her village. And yet the little village seemed too far away. As she reached the bottom of the stairs, her eyes noticed a familiar face. She looked again, and there on the lobby mirror was a small picture of her mother. Christina's eyes burned and her throat tightened as she walked across the room and removed the small photo. Written on the back was this message: "Whatever you have done, whatever you have become, it doesn't matter. Please come home." And Christina went home.[4]

Why is the gospel important? No one can truly come home in their spiritual life without Christ.

There is a God who longs to know us, and He made the first move. When Jesus died on the cross, it wasn't Plan B. God planned to rescue humanity all along with the gospel. Jesus is the "lamb without blemish and without spot . . . foreordained before the foundation of the world" (1 Peter 1:19–20, NKJV). The cross existed in the heart of God long before the universe was created.

Genesis 3 reveals so much to us about the gospel. Adam and Eve were in the garden along with two important trees. One, the tree of life, was there to sustain and serve as a reminder that in God's boundaries we will always find life. Once we get outside of His boundaries, death is sure to follow. The other tree, the tree of knowledge, was there as well. They were not to eat from that tree. Some ask "Why did God put two trees in the Garden of Eden? If God knew they would eat the fruit from the tree, why did God even create it? After all, didn't God create both trees?" Yes, God created both trees. Both trees are necessary. True love requires choice. The law says, "Don't put the tree of knowledge in the garden. Keep everyone away from it." Grace says, "Both trees belong in the garden." Grace requires and demands more from us than the law ever will.

Satan tempted Eve to eat from the forbidden tree. His tactic? First, he tried to cast doubt on God's truth. "Did God really say not to eat from that tree?" And second, he attacked her identity. "If you eat it, you will be like God." In other words, the way God created you isn't good enough. Do something else and become somebody else because you can't be satisfied the way God created you. Truth and identity were both maligned. Sound familiar?

Adam and Eve ate the fruit and didn't follow the path of God's best for their lives. By eating the fruit from the tree of knowledge, they invited death and spiritual separation into the world. What happened as a result? They immediately became full of shame. When they heard God coming into the garden, they hid. Why? They were naked and knew it. I once heard Erwin McManus say that they not only knew the sound of God's voice but the sound of His steps. They truly walked with God and yet chose to walk away. Upon discovering Adam and Eve in hiding, God had an unbelievably gracious conversation with them. In that moment, He could have punished them for violating His Word. I want to be clear. God did deal with their disobedience. He didn't ignore it. Grace doesn't overlook sin. Grace deals with it in a godly way. Sometimes grace tells someone the truth, like "Yes, you are naked and hiding, and you ate the fruit from the tree I commanded you not to eat from." Grace looks you and me in the face and shares the truth, even when it isn't politically correct. God removed Satan from the garden, and we catch a glimpse that God's solution for the disobedience of Adam and Eve is the gospel.

Genesis 3 introduces us to the indestructible and always relevant solution to the universal problem of death, sin, and separation from God. "I will put enmity between you [the serpent] and the woman, and between your offspring and hers; he will crush your head, and you will strike his heel" (Genesis 3:15). The gospel and only the gospel can bring those who are separated from God back to Him. God removed Satan from the garden. What about Adam and Eve? God clothed them. In the midst of their sin, while heartbroken, God reached out and covered their shame. This is amazing grace! He provided a spiritual solution for them in the cross of Christ long before their fall. God also met their practical needs as well. Just as God restored dignity to Nebuchadnezzar, Scripture tells us that God placed a flaming sword at the entrance of the Garden of Eden. Some read that and describe it as vengeance: "You blew it, God is mad at you, and now you can never enter into the garden again." But this wasn't an act of vengeance but an act of grace: "Although I love you, I don't want to take the risk that you will walk back into the garden and eat the fruit from the tree of life. For if you do, you will remain in your sinful state forever." God prevented them from returning to the garden because He loved them. Grace puts up boundaries even when people don't understand.

The fall of mankind in Genesis 3 is the apex of grace in the Old Testament, and it paves the way for the gospel to be expressed on the cross. The most important thing anyone can ever know is that there is a God who created us to know Him. Our sin separates us from Him and His purpose. Although we don't deserve His grace, He still extends it to us. Jesus died on the cross and paid the ultimate price for our sin (2 Corinthians 5:21). He was raised from the dead supernaturally and now intercedes on our behalf. Jesus came and lived a perfect life and died a horrific death. He is perfect theology. He isn't mad at you, and He isn't mad at the world. He will not, however, turn His face and pretend sin doesn't exist. We need Him to rescue us. The gospel is how we are rescued.

Unfortunately, many see the gospel as a "get out of hell for free card." Heaven and hell are real places. "Just as people are destined to die once, and after that to face judgment, so Christ was sacrificed once to take away the sins of many" (Hebrews 9:27–28). The gospel is much more than grace for judgment day.

The gospel provides identity to those who fall into peer pressure, are confused about who they really are, struggle with insecurity, or don't think their lives amount to much. "For you died, and your life is now hidden with Christ in God" (Colossians 3:3). That means your identity, who you really are, will never be fully realized until you know Jesus. This is true for everyone. Knowing that the God of the universe sings over you (Zephaniah 3) will certainly do something for your self-image.

The gospel enables people to see hope bloom in a hopeless situation. The gospel summons the dreamer from within to go through a difficult time rather than complain and run from it. How? "I can do all things through Christ who strengthens me" (Philippians 4:13, NKJV).

The gospel shows us there is more to life than making a lot of money or becoming popular. "You know the grace of our Lord Jesus Christ, that though he was rich, yet for your sake he became poor, so that you through his poverty might become rich" (2 Corinthians 8:9). "The Son of Man did not come to be served, but to serve, and to give his life as a ransom for many" (Mark 10:45). If God, who has everything He wants, chose to lay it all down to reveal the gospel, then our lives should be focused on this as well. True success isn't found in making a difference. It's found in making a difference with the gospel.

The gospel provides hope to the person who thinks God can't forgive them (Romans 8:1). The apostle Paul said, "Christ Jesus came into the world to save sinners—of whom I am the worst" (1 Timothy 1:15). Paul didn't ignore his sin or deny it. He accepted the facts but didn't stay there. He also accepted and embraced the grace of God. There are some horrible things going on in the world today. There are devastated people. While it is offensive to some, God can rescue even the darkest of souls. Nebuchadnezzar was responsible for a holocaust in ancient Israel; yet God forgave him and restored him. For the hopeless soul who feels condemned by God, the Bible tells us: "God demonstrates his own love for us in this: While we were still sinners, Christ died for us" (Romans 5:8).

There are countless multitudes who strive for God's approval through sacrifice, striving, and suffering. The gospel communicates that we can never be good enough or do enough. Salvation is free. "The wages of sin is death, but the gift of God is eternal life in Christ Jesus our Lord" (Romans 6:23).

Scripture is full of the gospel. Scripture is the gospel. God's primal burden is for us to be in relationship with Him. As humanity lies on the ground in pain and dying, like Joan Murray, there is a solution many people may not consider because, like the fire ants, it isn't even seen. The only way our world and the generations to come will ever know God is first and foremost through the gospel. This next generation will not be like the one in Judges 2. They will both know God and His works. I know this, because people like you are reading this book. In order to plant the seed of the gospel, we will need to plant another seed: the power of the Holy Spirit. The gospel compels us to live a life greater than ourselves. "Christ's love compels us, because we are convinced that one died for all, and therefore all died" (2 Corinthians 5:14). When we are compelled, we must go. But before we go, we need to receive the power of the Spirit . . . and the next generation needs to know why.

STUDENT QUESTIONS:

- How does our culture respond to the truth of Jesus being the only way to the Father?
- How are you finding strength in spending time with God, reading Scripture, and spending time in prayer?
- What difficult situation have you gone through that you saw God turn for good? Or, what are you going through now that you need to trust God and believe that what you see is not all there is?
- How effective is the time you spend reading, meditating on, and studying Scripture? What are your plans to improve in this area?

LEADER QUESTIONS:

- Are you preaching that Jesus is the only way to the Father? Do your students read the Bible enough to understand that He is not the best or preferred way, but the only way?
- What do you need to be doing in your quiet time with God to get from where you are to where He wants you to be?
- What tools are you offering to the next generation to inspire them to get into Scripture?
- Is it possible there are circumstances that you're avoiding concerning students in your ministry or your home? Ask God to reveal those to you.

CHAPTER FOUR

THE SEED OF THE SPIRIT

It is a story for a believing believer.

In the early '90s, Hawa Ahmed was a college student in North Africa. One day she received a Christian tract in her dorm room and accepted Christ. Because her father was opposed to her Christian faith, she knew he might disown her, but she was completely unprepared for what actually happened.

When she told her family that she had become a Christian and had changed her name to Faith, her father flew into a rage. He and her brothers stripped her naked, tied her to a chair, and put a big metal plate at her back, then wired it for 240 volts of electricity.

Faith begged them to put her Bible in her lap. Her father replied, "If you wish to die with your false teachings, so be it." A brother added, "This will prove your Christian teachings have no power."

Though her arms were tied, she was able to touch a corner of the Bible, and as she did, she felt a strange peace, as if someone were standing right beside her. They plugged in the cord—but nothing happened. They fiddled with the wires and tried four times, but the current refused to flow!

Finally, in frustration, the father beat her severely, screaming, "You are no longer my daughter!" and threw her into the street, still without a stitch of clothing. Bruised and disheveled, the once-beautiful girl ran through the streets in humiliation and pain. The humid African evening added to her feeling of hot embarrassment, though people did seem to look at her more in curiosity than in shock. Trembling and in tears, she ran all the way to the apartment of a Christian friend named Sarah.

Sarah's jaw dropped when she opened the door to see her naked, panting, wounded friend. She whisked Faith inside, clothed her, and tended to her needs. The next day, Sarah was speaking with several neighbors who told her they had seen Faith running up the street.

"Yes," Sarah commented, "how sad that my friend was thrown out of her home and forced to run through the streets unclothed."

"What are you talking about?" asked one of them.

"I'm talking about that young woman who ran naked to my door last night. She ran right past you."

"You must be mistaken. The girl who ran past us last night was wearing a beautiful white gown." The others agreed.

"Yes," added another, "we wondered why someone dressed so nicely was running down the street." Today, Faith is a full-time evangelist with Every Home for Christ.[5]

Apart from the mercy of God in protecting her and her deep commitment to serve Jesus Christ, I want you to catch the fact that her earthly reality didn't reveal all that there was. She was "clothed" with a spiritual reality that not everyone could see.

Jesus looked at the young adolescent disciples and said, "Follow me." They were a group of teenagers, overlooked by many and assumed to be too average for anything of significance in life, but Jesus saw them for who they could become. I can only imagine how amazing it was to be near someone like Jesus. Powerful enough for demons to tremble at His Word, yet gentle enough that even the smallest child wanted to be near Him.

Jesus said there was something better than being with Him. I know, it sounds awkward, but there it is in John 16:7: Jesus said to His disciples, "It is to your advantage that I go away" (ESV). To their advantage? What could be advantageous about being face-to-face with Jesus Himself only to have Him leave? Jesus went on to explain: "If I do not go away, the Helper will not come to you. But if I go, I will send him to you" (John 16:7, ESV).

Our relationship with the Father, made possible through the death and resurrection of Jesus Christ, grows through our interaction with the Holy Spirit. "The grace of the Lord Jesus Christ, and the love of God, and the fellowship of the Holy Spirit be with you all" (2 Corinthians 13:14). I'm grateful for the love of God. The grace found in the cross of Christ makes it possible for me to know Him. And the fellowship or deep friendship with the Holy Spirit is an honor, even better than being face-to-face with Jesus Himself.

When the townspeople saw Faith running through the streets clothed in white, it raises questions in my mind and I'm not completely sure what it means. It's a mystery, and only God knows all the answers. What I do know is that it portrays a great picture of what friendship looks like with the Holy Spirit. When we are filled with the Holy Spirit, we live and begin reflecting a reality that is much more real than anything we can see. The Holy Spirit doesn't just "clothe" us; He lives within us. This is a seed we must plant in the next generation:

how living in the power of the Holy Spirit is far greater than being with Jesus face-to-face.

WHO IS THE HOLY SPIRIT?

Who is the Holy Spirit and why is this so important? The Holy Spirit is God. He isn't an "it" or a "thing." He is a person, and He dwells in perfect unity with the Father and the Son.

We first meet the Holy Spirit in Genesis 1. The Spirit hovered over the chaos, in perfect peace, and God's creative work began. In a world of chaos, the Holy Spirit provides peace and creative perspective.

The first mention of anyone filled with the Spirit in Scripture is Exodus 31:2–4: "See, I have chosen Bezalel son of Uri, the son of Hur, of the tribe of Judah, and I have filled him with the Spirit of God, with wisdom, with understanding, with knowledge and with all kinds of skills—to make artistic designs for work in gold, silver and bronze." Notice that the first person who was filled with the Spirit wasn't a preacher, but an artist. Being filled with the Spirit isn't just for people who are "supposed to be spiritual." We can all encounter and experience the full impact of the Spirit in our lives. Bezalel was filled with the Spirit to put on earthly display in the tabernacle what God had already revealed from heaven. The Spirit helps us bring spiritual realities into our everyday lives.

Moses saw the impact of the Holy Spirit on someone's life and cried out prophetically in Numbers 11:29: "I wish that all the LORD's people were prophets and that the LORD would put His Spirit on them!" This prayer was later echoed in Joel's prophecy and the answer came in Acts 2 when the Spirit was poured out "on all people" (Joel 2:28). I wonder if those of us who are filled with the Holy Spirit are an answer to the prayer of Moses? Moses is the leader who cried out to God for His glory to be revealed (Exodus 33). His face glowed from being in the presence of God, yet he saw the importance of all of God's people being in relationship with the Holy Spirit.

Some heroes of old, like Gideon, were clothed with power from God's Spirit to lead (see Judges 6:34). There are some things our intellect and gifting cannot produce alone. We must not use prayer as an excuse to be lazy. Doing things with excellence honors the Lord; yet excellence isn't enough. We cannot fulfill God's plan for our lives by might or by power, but by His Spirit.

The first king of Israel, King Saul, was in relationship with the Holy Spirit. He was changed into a new person through the Spirit (1 Samuel 10:6) and began to lead God's people. Somewhere along the way, Saul became religious on the outside but spiritually cold on the inside. "The Spirit of the LORD . . . departed from Saul" (1 Samuel 16:14). While we want the power of the Spirit in our lives, He isn't for our entertainment or to make us better at what we do. The Spirit can take us places that our character must keep us. The Spirit wants to dwell among and within God's people; yet there are times when He leaves. May that never happen with us.

Joel prophesied about a time when all people would be introduced to the Spirit in a new way: "I will pour out my Spirit on all people. Your sons and daughters will prophesy, your old men will dream dreams, your young men will see visions" (Joel 2:28). For centuries the Spirit came upon individuals and left. But something special happened on the day John the Baptist baptized Jesus. "Then John gave this testimony: 'I saw the Spirit come down from heaven as a dove and remain on him'" (John 1:32).The Spirit remained on Jesus. What does it look like when the Spirit remains? Jesus lived a life that glorified the Father. He loved both friends and enemies. He spoke the truth even when it was unpopular. He wept over those who were lost and took a courageous stand with those who played religious games to their own benefit. We sometimes confuse being conservative with being holy; but holiness isn't old-fashioned. When our lives honor God and His Word, we can experience the presence of the Spirit in a breathtaking way.

John 3:34 tells us that God "gives the Spirit without limit." The Spirit who remained with Jesus during His entire earthly ministry is the same Spirit who comes into our lives today. There is no limit to how close we can be to God through the Spirit. We are in Christ, and He dwells in us (John 15:4). Since there are no limits, the only limits set are those we put in place. We are as close to God as we want to be.

Jesus told His disciples that it was to their benefit that He leave and send the Holy Spirit (John 16). The same Spirit who raised Christ from the dead lives within us (Romans 8:11). The same Spirit who was there in Genesis 1 lives within us. The same Spirit who clothed Gideon lives within us. The same Spirit Joel spoke of lives within us. And there is more.

Much more.

Jesus asked His disciples to remain in Jerusalem until the promise He alluded to many times would come. "You will receive power when the Holy Spirit comes on you; and you will be my witnesses" (Acts 1:8). Witnesses of what? Witnesses of Jesus. The disciples had received the

Holy Spirit (John 20:22), but Jesus knew they would need more than that to be witnesses of the gospel: they would need to be baptized in the Holy Spirit. That is why Jesus instructed them: "I am going to send you what my Father has promised; but stay in the city [Jerusalem] until you have been clothed with power from on high" (Luke 24:49).

That is what happened when the disciples were gathered in the upper room in Jerusalem. A sound like a rushing wind filled the room, and the 120 people gathered there began to speak in foreign languages. They were filled with mighty Holy Spirit power that gave them the courage to travel throughout the known world and preach the gospel as witnesses to the resurrection of Jesus Christ. The Holy Spirit enables us to encounter God time and time again so we become witnesses, not necessarily of what we believe, but witnesses of who and how we believe. It is about Jesus and His resurrection from the dead.

We serve a God who can do all things. "[He] is able to do immeasurably more than all we ask or imagine, according to his power that is at work within us" (Ephesians 3:20). What a promise! That power "within us" is the Holy Spirit. And much of what God does in and through our lives is closely linked to how we cultivate our friendship with the Spirit. For the sake of our families, our churches, and our communities, we must plant in the hearts of the next generation the seed of spiritual awakening through a relationship with Holy Spirit. They need to know why the baptism in the Spirit and praying in a heavenly language are important. We are called to live supernatural lives, but we cannot do this without power from on high.

Jesus' instruction to be baptized in the Holy Spirit is not a call to be weird or to overreact. It's a summons to remember that Scripture is filled with a God who does wonders and performs miracles. A God who is less concerned with being accused of being weird and much more concerned that His kingdom come to earth through people like us. There are clear guidelines in Scripture for spiritual gifts to be exercised in decency and in order. Sometimes I wonder if our sincere desire to honor this biblical mandate causes the Spirit to feel unwelcome among us. If we aren't careful, we will talk about a God who stands on the other side of the door knocking, while those of us inside celebrate and do ministry, never noticing He isn't even in our midst (see Revelation 3:20). He is knocking, but we can't hear His knock over the sound of our songs and our sermons.

Jesus didn't promise the Advocate of the Holy Spirit just so we could preach better and lead better. The Holy Spirit is a third member of the triune Godhead. He is holy. He demonstrates the kingdom. His gifts reveal a God who can heal the sick, encourage the depressed, bring healing to broken marriages, and grant wisdom to parents who don't know where to begin raising their kids. He provides a song in the night when we have no hope. He tells us the truth and convicts us of the right path to walk in an age where many versions of "truth" are pushed off on us. He opens our eyes to see the Word of God as Scripture is illuminated. He comforts us. He prays with us. He always points us to Jesus.

Jesus is our example. Wherever He went, hell trembled and sickness left; yet children felt safe enough to be near Him. This is the pattern worth following. Our lives must be so filled with the presence of the Holy Spirit that hell notices and fears while children feel safe and at home.

Does your life make sense when you put it inside the Bible? Isaiah 60:1 says, "Arise, shine, for your light has come, and the glory of the LORD rises upon you." We don't arise and hide. We don't arise and run for the hills. We don't arise and create a subculture to hide in. We don't even arise and reflect. We arise and shine.

Let a hunger for the presence of the Holy Spirit and a growing relationship with Jesus through the Spirit lead you to approach the Father in bold prayer. Perhaps your passion for Him was stronger in the past. Rather than being ashamed or embarrassed, let this serve as a reminder that God longs to encounter you as much as you want to encounter Him. Today could be the beginning of a fresh outpouring of the Spirit in your life. Regardless of how long the seed has been dormant, let's pray and believe for the seed of Pentecost to be planted again in our soil. Trust me, it will bloom.

For thousands of years, Judean date palm trees were one of the most recognizable and welcome sights for people in the Middle East.[6] Widely cultivated throughout the region for their sweet fruit, they also offered a cool shade from the blazing desert sun. From its founding some three thousand years ago to the current age, the trees became a staple crop in the Kingdom of Judea. Judean palm trees became one of the kingdom's chief symbols of good fortune; King David named his daughter, Tamar, after the plant's name in Hebrew.

At the time the Roman Empire sought to usurp control of the kingdom in AD 70, broad forests of the palms flourished as a staple crop in the Judean economy—a fact that made them a prime resource for invading armies to destroy. Sadly, by the year AD 500, the once plentiful palm had been completely wiped out, driven to extinction for the sake of conquest.

In the centuries that followed, firsthand knowledge of the tree slipped from memory to legend. Until recently, that is.

During excavations at the site of Herod the Great's palace in Israel in the early 1960s, archeologists unearthed a small stockpile of seeds stowed in a clay jar dating back two thousand years. For the next four decades, the ancient seeds were kept in a drawer at Tel Aviv's Bar-Ilan University. But then, in 2005, botanical researcher Elaine Solowey decided to plant one of the seeds to see if it would sprout.[7] "I assumed the food in the seed would be no good after all that time. How could it be?" Solowey commented. She was soon proven wrong.

Amazingly, the multimillennial seed did indeed sprout—producing a sapling no one had seen in centuries to become the oldest-known tree seed to germinate. Today, the living archeological treasure continues to grow and thrive. In 2011, it even produced its first flower; a heartening sign that the ancient survivor was eager to reproduce.

The amazing way that ancient date palm seed came to life fills me with hope. In a similar way, I pray that the ancient "seed" of the power of the Holy Spirit that often lies dormant among our churches would be planted in the hearts of young people to spring to life once again. This was the seed buried deep in the heart of the teenage Sister Carney that was nurtured in prayer to bloom in a mighty revival of Holy Spirit power at the turn of the twentieth century. Jesus did not promise that His disciples alone would receive this Holy Spirit power. The promise is for us and for our children: "The promise is for you and your children and for all who are far off—for all whom the Lord our God will call" (Acts 2:39). This seed still works. This seed can still grow. We need to plant it and watch it bloom again!

STUDENT QUESTIONS:

- How is your relationship with the Holy Spirit? Do you treat the Holy Spirit more like a power or a person?

- How are you making the most of having the Holy Spirit with you wherever you go?

- Galatians 5:22–23 (ESV) says, "But the fruit of the Spirit is love, joy, peace, patience, kindness, goodness, faithfulness, gentleness, self-control." Which fruit of the Spirit do you see in your life?

- How open are you to the power and miracles of the Holy Spirit working in your life, school, friendships, and home?

LEADER QUESTIONS:

- In which areas of your personal life, your home, and your ministry are you allowing or not allowing the Holy Spirit to work?

- How active is the Holy Spirit in your life? How often do you experience an increased awareness of the Spirit in areas outside of your private life?

- How are you modeling and training the next generation to depend on the Holy Spirit?

- When was the last time you encouraged your students to ask for the gifts of the Holy Spirit?

CHAPTER FIVE

THE SEED OF THE MISSION

I don't know if he arose to the pitter-patter of rain or if the cool breeze greeted him through the window. What I do know is that while others were sleeping or resting, he was on the move. The further he walked the more urgency he felt. According to the story James Rutz refers to in his book *Megashift,*[8] an Indian evangelist named Sadhu Chellappa was sleeping in a small village to the north of Madras when he was suddenly wide awake. Immediately, upon waking, his heart began to pound and he sensed an overwhelming burden to leave the house where he was staying and run away. Quickly! So, he started running.

If someone had passed him on the street at such a late hour they might have asked, "Why are you running?"

Chellappa would have responded, "I have no idea."

"Oh, okay, well, where are you going? Do you need a ride?" the innocent bystander might have asked.

"I have no idea where I'm going. I only know that God woke me up and told me to run."

I'm sure that would have brought the conversation to an abrupt end. "God woke you up? God told you to run? Kids, stay away from that man. He's creepy."

There was nothing convenient about it. I'm sure Chellappa was exhausted from his missions trip. But, as he later recounted, he was used to receiving unique and inconvenient directions from the Lord. That night he was running into the darkness in remote India to a place he did not know.

In the open country, away from the dim lights of the village fires, he passed a large tree. In that moment, he sensed God wanted him to stop and begin preaching the gospel. Chellappa did just that. With nobody in sight and nothing but an open field for a congregation, he proclaimed the grace of Jesus Christ. At the end of his message, he gave opportunity for anyone who could potentially hear him to open their hearts to Christ's forgiveness. In the darkness, sobbing echoed through the open field as the tree branches parted above Chellappa's head. Without hesitation, a man who was at the top of the tree quickly climbed down and, with tear-stained cheeks, gave his life to Christ. When Chellappa asked what in the world the man was doing at the top of the tree in the middle of nowhere, the man confessed, "I came here to hang myself."

What an amazing story of immediate obedience! And how remarkable that God loved that man so much, God woke a perfect stranger in the middle of the night to run to a tree and share a message of hope with him. I'm not sure what happened to the man, but I do know that neither he nor Chellappa will ever forget that moment.

I picture heaven standing at attention while the man climbs the tree with a rope in his hand. The angels are wondering who will be faith-filled enough and willing to say yes to a summons from God that doesn't make a lot of sense. What would our response be to such a summons? Today God is calling us to serve humanity. Heaven could trust Chellappa with such an assignment. Heaven trusts us with the same: "Therefore go and make disciples of all nations, baptizing them in the name of the Father and of the Son and of the Holy Spirit" (Matthew 28:19). Notice that Jesus doesn't call us to make converts. After all, He didn't come to earth to create Christianity. He came because "there is no other name under heaven given to mankind by which we must be saved" (Acts 4:12). He calls us to go and make disciples.

It doesn't take a lot of imagination to wonder what would have happened to the man in the tree had no one been willing to say yes to what God asked. There are many others, like the man in the tree, who have no one to come to them in the darkness with the gospel and in the power of the Spirit. They perish without knowing Jesus. The greatest injustice in all of the earth is for someone to live and die without knowing Christ. This is the most basic human right.

In the previous chapter, we emphasized the need to plant the seed of the power of the Holy Spirit in the next generation. We need the power of the Spirit to effectively preach and, even more so, to demonstrate the gospel of Jesus Christ. Like that father on the edge of the Sahel, I'm asking you to take the future by the hand one more time and walk up and down the field and plant this seed yet again. The climate may not seem conducive to produce a harvest and the dirt may be ever dry. That didn't stop our Heavenly Father when He planted Jesus, a "root out of dry ground" in a barren culture. If we aren't personally engaged in the story of God, our spiritual experiences are destitute and empty. May we slow down long enough, even if we are on the way to prayer, to notice the generation God has placed in our path. That's what Peter and John did.

Now Peter and John were going up to the temple at the hour of prayer, the ninth hour. And a man lame from birth was being carried, whom they laid daily at the gate of the temple that is called the Beautiful Gate to ask alms of those entering the temple. Seeing Peter and John about to go into the temple, he asked to receive alms. And Peter directed his gaze at him, as did John, and said, "Look at us." And he fixed his attention on them, expecting to receive something from them. But Peter said, "I have no silver and gold, but what I do have I give to you. In the name of Jesus Christ of Nazareth, rise up and walk!" And he took him by the right hand and raised him up, and immediately his feet and ankles were made strong. And leaping up, he stood and began to walk, and entered the temple with them, walking and leaping and praising God. And all the people saw him walking and praising God, and recognized him as the one who sat at the Beautiful Gate of the temple, asking for alms. And they were filled with wonder and amazement at what had happened to him.

While he clung to Peter and John, all the people, utterly astounded, ran together to them in the portico called Solomon's. And when Peter saw it he addressed the people: "Men of Israel, why do you wonder at this, or why do you stare at us, as though by our own power or piety we have made him walk? The God of Abraham, the God of Isaac, and the God of Jacob, the God of our fathers, glorified his servant Jesus, whom you delivered over and denied in the presence of Pilate, when he had decided to release him. But you denied the Holy and Righteous One, and asked for a murderer to be granted to you, and you killed the Author of life, whom God raised from the dead. To this we are witnesses. And his name— by faith in his name—has made this man strong whom you see and know, and the faith that is through Jesus has given the man this perfect health in the presence of you all." (Acts 3:1–16, ESV)

In this story we see the basic concepts of the gospel collide: the Spirit, justice, compassion, and the right to know Jesus. Overlooked by many, a lame beggar teaches us how to truly walk with God. The timid communicator Peter, who denied Jesus by the fire in the courtyard of the high priest, went out of his way to help the lame man, not for the allure of the crowd but for the beauty found in the eyes of one individual who had the right to know Jesus.

Who is Jesus? The Son of an obscure Jewish carpenter, Jesus never traveled more than one hundred miles from His hometown. He was a Hebrew who spoke Aramaic, and yet His teachings are recorded in Greek. Jesus is the Son of God, born of a virgin, who lived a perfect, sinless life. He came teaching, not what to think but how to think. He voluntarily laid His life down and died in our place for our sin before the holy and perfect Father. He was resurrected from the dead and more than five hundred eyewitnesses saw Him after the resurrection. Jesus is not a fairy tale. He is a literal person, and His crucifixion and resurrection are historical facts. Jesus slowed down and noticed Peter, and Peter did the same for the beggar.

It's my prayer that you would never abort a miracle in someone else's life simply because you don't think God can use you. Don't allow insecurity or fear to rob someone else of an opportunity to know Jesus. Let them make the decision whether or not they want to embrace the gospel. In your insecurity, fear, laziness, or apathy, don't make that decision for them.

What is the crux of Peter's experience with the lame man? In order to understand what was going on in the temple courtyard, we need to go back to the Feast of Pentecost when many of the Jews witnessed the power and love of Jesus firsthand, hearing the wonders of God declared in their own language. The 120 disciples saw the fire rest upon the heads of the others in the prayer meeting, they heard the tongues, felt a literal shaking, and encountered a sound like a violent wind in the room. They experienced physical proof that Jesus Christ is who He says He is.

A key to the outpouring of the Holy Spirit during the Feast of Pentecost in Acts 2 is found in verse 14: "Then Peter stood up with the Eleven, raised his voice and addressed the crowd: 'Fellow Jews and all of you who live in Jerusalem, let me explain this to you; listen carefully to what I say.'" After Peter spoke to God in an unknown tongue, he spoke to hundreds of people in a known tongue, in a relevant way that all of them could understand. God-encounters must translate into practical living, practical ministry, and practical acts of love. Peter is our example: The more spiritual we are, the more practical we become.

MIRACLES AMONG THE ORDINARY

Every day we come in contact with a crippled generation of people who are begging for help that only Jesus and His Holy Spirit can provide. It is my prayer that you would never sabotage, overlook, or abort the miraculous simply because the circumstance seems too familiar. We learn this lesson from a small child.

At the turn of the twentieth century, a little girl stood near a small church, where she had been turned away because it was too crowded. The pastor happened to walk past and heard her crying. It was obvious that she came from a poor home. Her clothes were torn and tattered. She wasn't the type of person to attend such a prestigious church. The pastor took her by the hand and walked her to Sunday school and placed her in a seat. The young girl had the time of her life, and that night went to bed thinking about all the little children who had no place to worship Jesus. Two years later, the girl's body was found lifeless. Poverty and illness had taken their toll on the little life. Her parents called the pastor who had befriended her to handle the funeral arrangements. When they moved her little body they found a stained, tattered red purse beside her. Inside was fifty-seven cents and a note that read: "This is to help build the little church bigger so more children can go to Sunday school."

For two years, she had been saving this offering of love. The pastor was touched by the faith and compassion of someone who could have excused her gift as too small or could rightly have claimed that she had nothing to give. He read the note to the congregation and challenged the deacons to get busy raising money for a larger building. A newspaper got ahold of the story and published it. When a wealthy realtor read the article he offered the church a choice piece of property worth thousands of dollars. When they asked the realtor the price of the land, he responded, "Fifty-seven cents." People from all over began to give to the project, and soon the little girl's fifty-seven cents grew into over $250,000, a massive sum one hundred years ago. If you are ever in Philadelphia, look up Temple Baptist Church, which seats 3,300, and Temple University, where hundreds of students are trained. Have a good look too at the Good Samaritan Hospital and the large Sunday school building, large enough so all the children in the neighborhood can come. And as you walk down the hallway of that Sunday school building, slow down just enough to notice the picture of the sweet face of that little girl who took her meager fifty-seven cents and placed it in God's hands, where it multiplied many times over![9]

There are miracles shrouded as ordinary conversations, ordinary events, and ordinary people. Like the little girl and like Peter and John, the miraculous can occur when we simply pay attention to who and what is in our path.

Peter and John, along with many other believers, were going to the temple. The Temple Mount, the platform on which the temple was built, was about the size of fifteen football fields. The temple was made of white marble and intricately laden with gold. The building caught everybody's attention. Everyone could enter into what was called the Courtyard of the Gentiles. Beyond the courtyard was a gate through which only Jews could pass. The Beautiful Gate was in the outer courtyard. There the beggar could sit close to where the priests would go in and meet with God. Little did the beggar know that God was right there with him all along.

Notice a few key elements in this story. Peter and John went to the temple at the hour of prayer. There is substantial evidence that the New Testament church folded prayer into the rhythm of their lives. I heard the quote once that "prayerlessness is the ultimate pride." When someone is a person of prayer, they reflect the face of the One they look toward. When someone is a person of prayer, the focus on reaching the world with the gospel is strengthened. Show me someone who isn't concerned with those who are spiritually lost and away from Christ and I will show you someone who doesn't truly pray. "Whoever dwells in the shelter of the Most High will rest in the shadow of the Almighty" (Psalm 91:1). Acts 5:15–16 tells us that people brought the sick to the streets so that Peter's shadow could pass over them and heal them. The people believed that an anointing from God extended as far as your shadow. But we know that Peter's shadow did not heal anyone; God's shadow healed them. Peter learned how to dwell in the secret place and abide under "the shadow of the Almighty" God. Prayer doesn't make a difference; it makes *the* difference.

Peter said to the lame man, "Silver or gold I do not have." The Acts 2 church had all things in common. Peter could easily have found some coins to give to the man, but his gaze was fixed on something more important: the gospel. Peter knew that the man needed to be healed far more than he needed a coin. The beggar needed the gospel. Peter recognized the human right of this beggar to know Jesus and took it upon himself to make Jesus known.

Peter took the beggar by the right hand. To separate the gospel from acts of compassion only results in a better brand of misery for the lost. To separate compassion from the gospel is to preach a gospel Jesus never preached. The gospel and compassion go hand in hand. Peter took the beggar by the right hand and helped him up. I see here a clear emphasis not on justice, but on compassion. The miracle was complete and the man was healed. The compassion in Peter's heart led him to reach out and help the healed beggar stand up. God places immense value on community and belonging. In some moments something as simple as taking someone by the hand is a profound display of God's power at work. The gospel was never intended merely to be preached, but to be demonstrated through the power of miracles, the practicality of taking someone by the hand, fueled by the compassion of the heart. Peter offered Jesus to the beggar: not enough of Jesus to be forgiven, but to be transformed. The man was touched physically (walking), emotionally (leaping), and spiritually (praising God.)

The simple act of noticing the physical and spiritual condition led to a miracle of healing and salvation. This, then, led to preaching the gospel to a large group of people. In Acts 4:4, about five thousand men heard the gospel and were saved. Peter could never have imagined thousands of people responding to the gospel on that day simply because he slowed down long enough to notice a beggar. An impoverished little girl could never have imagined the impact of her fifty-seven cents. Chellappa could never have known the eternal impact of his obedience when he arose in the middle of the night and shared the gospel under a tree in a field under a dark sky. And as you read this, let me remind you that your obedience in prayer and sacrificial giving to missions goes well beyond any impact you could fathom.

The beggar was hopeless until Peter and John came to him. This is an appeal for local evangelism and frontier missions. It's our mandate to take the gospel to those who have yet to hear; to tell them of the love of God and to show them the love of God. It reminds me of some wonderful quotes from missions pioneers.

Robert Moffat said, "In the vast plain to the north I have sometimes seen, in the morning sun, the smoke of a thousand villages where no missionary has ever been."

Dave Davidson said, "World missions was on God's mind from the beginning."

Oswald J. Smith said, "We talk of the second coming; half of the world has never heard of the first."

John Falconer said, "I have but one candle of life to burn, and I would rather burn it out in a land filled with darkness than in a land flooded with light."

Mike Stachura said, "The mark of a great church is not its seating capacity, but its sending capacity."

J. Hudson Taylor said, "Would that God would make hell so real to us that we cannot rest; heaven so real that we must have men there."

William Booth said, "'Not *called*,' did you say? Not *heard* the call, I think you should say. He has been calling loudly ever since He spoke your sins forgiven—if you are forgiven at all—entreating and beseeching you to be His ambassador. Put your ear down to the Bible, and hear Him bid you go and pull poor sinners out of the fire of sin. Put your ear down to the burdened, agonized, heart of humanity, and listen to its pitying wail for help. Go and stand by the gates of Hell, and hear the damned entreat you to go to their father's house, and bid their brothers, and sisters, and servants, and masters not to come there. And then look the Christ in the face, whose mercy you profess you have got, and whose words you have promised to obey, and tell Him whether you will join us heart and soul and body and circumstances in this march to publish His mercy to all the world."

We hold close the responsibility to take the next generation by the hand and model why we serve in the harvest field. We must plant the seed of missions and equip the next generation to be personally engaged in sharing the love of God with the lost, whether around the corner or around the world. Being personally responsible isn't always convenient or popular, but it is necessary. Just ask Tilly.

Triggered by an earthquake that erupted on the ocean's floor, December 26, 2004, the Indian Ocean tsunami devastated coastal areas in twelve countries and killed more than 230,000 people. One story that emerged from the rubble was of a ten-year-old British girl named Tilly Smith. Tilly was on holiday with her family on the Thai island of Phuket. She had learned in her geography class that the phenomenon of water suddenly receding from the beach was always a symptom that a tsunami was about to strike. She told her mother about this and the news spread, allowing hundreds of people to evacuate Maikhao beach and a neighboring hotel before the ocean water swept in. Just elementary science and a wonderfully perceptive girl saved hundreds of lives. One person can stop the cries of pain.

Let's plant the seed of missions in the soil of the future so that other "Tillys" will lift up their voices and stop the pain.

STUDENT QUESTIONS:

- How important is it that we obey God even if it doesn't make sense?
- What patterns or routines in your life are blocking you from hearing God?
- As we assume our responsibility in the mission of God, what is something you can do this week to share God's love?
- How would your life look different if your time, money, and talents were focused on the mission of God?

LEADER QUESTIONS:

- When was the last time you heard God's voice, and did you respond? Why or why not?
- As a parent or leader, what is your greatest fear in obeying God's voice? How do you plan to overcome that?
- Do you tend to celebrate big results or big faith?
- How is your prayer life and sacrificial giving in line with the mission of God?

EPILOGUE

Long after I finished the book *The Bush Always Burns*, I noticed something in Deuteronomy 33. Honestly, my first thought was *Why didn't I see this before the book was finished? It's the perfect ending.* It became apparent that it was to my benefit that I didn't notice it until after the book was complete. Sometimes God shares things with us that are just for us. Some things aren't supposed to be shared. At least, not right away. But now I think it's appropriate to share it with you.

As Moses neared the end of his days, the future of his people was on his mind. He was not to enter the Promised Land though he was aware of the blessings and battles that lay ahead for the people. You can tell a lot about a person by their last words. When someone leaves office, their final speech says a lot about them as a person. On a deathbed, when someone is stepping from this life into the next one, they think clearly and coherently of what is to be said. Last words often summarize much of what a person seldom spoke but carried deep in their heart.

With the end of his life in sight, Moses pronounced a blessing over the various tribes of Israel. "About Joseph he said: 'May the LORD bless his land with the precious dew from heaven above and with the deep waters that lie below; with the best the sun brings forth and the finest the moon can yield; with the choicest gifts of the ancient mountains and the fruitfulness of the everlasting hills; with the best gifts of the earth and its fullness and *the favor of him who dwelt in the burning bush'*" (Deuteronomy 33:13–16, emphasis added).

There are times in Scripture when God is revealed or known by a new name. This is one of them. It doesn't change who He is; after all, He doesn't change (Malachi 3:6), and He is the same yesterday, today, and forever (Hebrews 13:8). It does reveal an aspect of Him we might have overlooked or ignored. Moses encountered the One who inhabited the ordinary. Moses encountered the One who revealed Himself in a barren and often uninhabited place. Moses noticed the God who speaks after He watches His servants turn aside to see.

Moses passed down a legacy to many people. He is the one who dared to believe God for freedom from the strong arm of Pharaoh. He is the one who combined prayer with action when he stretched out his rod and watched God part the Red Sea. He is the one who pulled away from the crowd and accepted God's invitation for divine encounter. He redefined law and order when he taught the Ten Commandments. He slowed down long enough to notice God at work in the burning bush and from that encounter, Moses created a new vocabulary to describe the never-changing One.

Have you encountered God in a profound way? A way so breathtaking that you have no words to describe Him? Has there been a moment in your life recently when you realized your world was aflame with God? And if so, are you going to pass this down to the next generation?

The greatest legacy we can leave is one of encounter. It's that moment when the ceiling of our faith becomes the floor of the next generation's. As you look to the future and pray, I hope you long to encounter God in spiritual and practical ways. I hope that what you have experienced and, more importantly, who you have encountered propels you for their sakes. Like Moses. In many ways, like Robert Woodruff.

On May 8, 1886, the very first Coca-Cola beverage was sold in Atlanta, Georgia. No one could have predicted that a worldwide legacy was about to be born.

Especially because originally Coke wasn't a success. In the first year, Coca-Cola brought in fifty dollars in revenue with seventy dollars in operating expenses. It didn't take long to figure out that the Coca-Cola company wasn't going to last if something didn't change.

The answer was Robert Woodruff. In 1926, at the age of thirty-seven, Woodruff became the president of the fledgling company. Although he certainly brought organization and focus, as well as business practices and marketing principles, to drive the company forward, one particular statement stands out to me as paramount. He said, "In my generation, it is my desire that everyone in the world have a taste of Coca-Cola." Almost one hundred years later, Woodruff's goal has basically been fulfilled, though he didn't live to see it.[10]

Today, Coca-Cola owns over half of all soft drinks sold around the world. The annual revenue of Coke is over $47 billion. The company has employees worldwide and each day 1.8 billion Coke bottles are sold while 10,450 Coke drinks are consumed each second.

If you were to take all of the Coke ever produced and package it in the same bottles it originally came in, they would stretch from the earth to the moon and back around two thousand times. I have been told that around 90 percent of the world can recognize the Coke brand. In fact, I have been in places where I was the first American to ever shake the hand of a villager, but there was a Coke banner over the window of the local store or hut. How does a company go from selling twenty-five bottles the first year and fighting bankruptcy, to selling 10,450 per second?

If you ask me, the answer is that one person had a vision and a passion. One person broke the silence and shared a goal. One person dared to dream and submitted his voice to a new conversation. And one person—Robert Woodruff—set his sights on the impossible, so that no one would die without tasting Coke. If this is possible with one person, imagine what could be possible if an entire generation of people submitted themselves to God's purpose and planted good seed so the next generation would live off of good fruit.

What if we were as passionate about spreading love as Robert Woodruff was about spreading "enjoyment"? What if our zeal for sharing a taste of the Spirit matched Woodruff's for sharing a taste of Coke? What if we "tasted and saw" that the Lord was good? What if we marched forward with one single desire in mind, to share just a taste of Jesus with the world? This is what Jesus had in mind when He made the promise in Acts 1:8. Once we taste the promise of the Father, we cannot keep Him to ourselves.

It's my prayer that we would say unequivocally that it is our desire, that in our generation and the next, everyone would have a taste of the gospel, the Spirit, and God's mission to love and save the world.

Until all know.

STUDENT QUESTIONS:

- In what ways are you open to God revealing Himself to you?
- Who, parent or leader, has the authority to speak into your life and challenge you to grow spiritually?
- How has your experience with God impacted your identity and purpose?
- How passionate are you about spreading the gospel until all know?

LEADER QUESTIONS:

- In what ways are you gospel centered, Spirit empowered, and personally responsible? In what areas are you struggling to be gospel-centered, Spirit-empowered, and personally-responsible?
- Is your relationship with Christ and your knowledge of Him and His works something that you would want to pass on to the next generation?
- How passionate are you about planting the seeds of the gospel, the Spirit, and the mission until all know?
- How will that passion affect the way you live your life? How will it affect the way you lead in your home and in your ministry?

NOTES

1. The information about Jericho has been compiled from multiple sources and notes gathered over the years.

2. Tommy Welchel, *True Stories of the Miracles of Azusa Street and Beyond* (Shippensburg, PA: Destiny Image, 2013), 37–49.

3. https://www.elitereaders.com/woman-skydiver-survived-fall-14500-feet-bitten-fire-ants/

4. Max Lucado, *No Wonder They Call Him the Savior* (Nashville: Thomas Nelson, 1986), 137–139.

5. This story was told to me by Dick Eastman. It took place during his years of ministry with Every Home for Christ.

6. http://www.treehugger.com/natural-sciences/extinct-tree-grows-anew-after-archaeologists-dig-ancient-seed-stockpile.html

7. http://news.nationalgeographic.com/news/051122-old-plant-seed-food/

8. James Rutz, *Megashift* (Colorado Springs, CO: Empowerment Press, 2005), 4–5.

9. http://www.turnbacktogod.com/story-how-temple-baptist-church-philadelphia-came-into-being/ (Story details vary by source.)

10. https://en.wikipedia.org/wiki/Robert_W._Woodruff

ABOUT THE AUTHOR

At the age of seventeen, Heath's life was dramatically transformed by an encounter with Jesus. Heath is the product of one person who believed in a promise, and who continually prayed for him. Years later, Heath married that one person. Heath and his wife, Ali, endeavor to leave a legacy for generations to come. They have two daughters.

Heath is the senior director of Youth Ministries for the General Council of the Assemblies of God. With a growing global platform, Heath also chairs the World Assemblies of God Fellowship Next Generation Commission and co-chairs Empowered 21's Next Generation Network.

Heath is the author of *The Bush Always Burns*. His undergraduate work occurred at North Central University and his graduate work at Evangel University. He is a PhD candidate in Religious Studies at Chester University.